WHEREVER WE FLOa., ...

POEMS BY MAYA TEVET DAYAN
TRANSLATED FROM THE HEBREW
BY JANE MEDVED

saturnalia | BOOKS

Distributed by Independent Publishers Group
Chicago

Saturnalia Books
2816 North Kent Rd.
Broomall, PA 19008
info@saturnaliabooks.com

ISBN: 978-1-947817-70-8 (print), 978-1-947817-71-5 (ebook)
Library of Congress Control Number: 2024935290

Cover art and book design by Robin Vuchnich

Distributed by:
Independent Publishing Group
814 N. Franklin St.
Chicago, IL 60610

CONTENTS

III. Winter

IV. SPRING

For Harel—
My Home and Land

Author's Introduction: Toward Life

I wrote these poems in a rainforest in Western Canada, on islands, along roads, on top of mountains. I was a mother of two, then three. We created a self-sufficient lifestyle, crafting our own food and cosmetics, growing some of it, parenting, moving from place to place, wandering far from familiarity, language, and family. We became complete strangers to our usual selves.

This nomadic life was my way of grieving the loss of my mother and along with it, the loss of any sense of home in the world. Instead, I transformed the entire world into a home, a motion that commemorated my mother's free-spirited nature. Hers was a brand new death. In "death years" she was like a baby in its early stages. And just as pregnant women *eat* for their fetuses, I felt that now I had the responsibility to *live* for the two of us.

Although I wrote these poems as a poetic journal of those years in our lives, they serve as a map for all who grieve, who seek a place in the world, who ask where they belong, who have lost a home, who still believe in beauty; those whose lives have sent them to float, willingly or unwillingly, and instead of sinking into sorrow, decide to say to life one short word: *OK.*

This book is my *OK* to life.

Maya Tevet Dayan

Translator's Notes: A Shift in Perspective

I first met Maya Tevet Dayan in a crowded café in Tel Aviv. I had translated a few of her poems, but I wanted to see if we had enough chemistry to make a longer project work. Surrounded by the hiss of espresso machines and conversations, we read poems back and forth to each other. Maya read the Hebrew. I responded with the English translation. The cadence, rhythm, and intensity of the words all fit together. We were speaking in two languages, but with the same voice. Translation was our bridge between cultures. But the overriding themes of motherhood, loss, family, alienation, and belonging were universal.

The speaker in this collection is a wife, but also a wanderer; a woman who freely admits that she can't stay put, either as a teenage girl or a mother of three. A cultivated restlessness infuses the book, as the narrator continually tries to find her place in the world. At times, this instability is traced back to relatives who were caught by the Holocaust. But in poems such as "Australia," it is simply the speaker's need for an ever-widening horizon, her addiction to the constant state of possibility.

Generations of women inhabit Tevet Dayan's work, where relationships are not bounded by the physical universe. Grandmothers, great-grandmothers, and her own mother, who died from cancer, advise, admonish, and applaud her throughout these poems. They form "the transparent generations / of mothers and daughters who rose / and slept their lives between light and darkness / from sleep to awakening to sleep" ("My Daughter is the Gateway to the Night"). They hand down wisdom, argue with each other, and suggest that the speaker might want to wash the floor. The kitchen table, a pot of soup, the dog's wet nose—this is the stuff of the poet's magical world, as she ponders reincarnation and the growing piles of laundry with equal passion.

Perhaps the strongest narrative thread in this collection is the illness and early death of Tevet Dayan's mother, a loss she is still writing about. Sometimes the speaker is herself a mother, sometimes a motherless child. Sometimes she is both at once, confronting the terrible responsibility of love. Time and place may change, but the focus remains the same: family, with its constraints and opportunities, will both protect and restrict you. Family defines you. And family allows you to grow.

Tevet Dayan's work is rich with myth, fable, apocryphal stories, family legend, and biblical allusions. She warns us that women can be turned into trees, that karma must be accumulated, and that souls will come back to visit. She reminds us that the universe is perched precariously, there are unequal measures of light and dark, but we ourselves are "immaculate and wondering" ("Nativity").

What attracted me the most to these poems was Tevet Dayan's creation of parallel and sometimes conflicting realities: childhood innocence masks loss and trauma, the present is inhabited by messengers from the past, the familiar becomes strange, and the strange is revealed to be expected and commonplace. Nothing can be taken for granted, since reality is not a solid platform, but a living entity, layered and shifting. This is a world of the seen and the unseen, where the physical and spiritual are on equal footing.

Oddly enough (or perhaps not), this shifting of perspectives mirrors the Hebrew language itself. Hebrew is built upon three letter linguistic "roots" which then branch out into different directions. Thus, you can have the word for "weapon" (נשק) coming out of the same root as the word for "kiss" (נשיקה)—a commentary on the nature of sexuality. Or the word for "before" (קדם) coming from the same root as "onwards" (קדימה)—a reflection on the interdependence between past and future. The ear of the Hebrew speaker is attuned to these nuances, which are sometimes impossible to recreate.

In the poem "Genealogy," we came across an instance of this. The poem is about the speaker's almost genetic need to wander "inherited" from relatives who were caught and died in the Holocaust. At the end of the poem the speaker returns to her family, where her daughter waves a handwritten sign. On the sign, her child's unintentional spelling mistake has turned "Welcome Home" into "Welcome Escapee." We circled this line for years, but nothing quite captured the irony of the original. Ultimately, we cut that poem from the manuscript.

As in any translation, some things simply don't cross over. The title of "Rehabilitation," for example, in the original Hebrew was "The Fighter's House." In Hebrew the phrase plays off of multiple cultural and semantic associations that are almost unconscious to an Israeli reader. In English, and especially to Americans, it has different associations. We decided to forgo the original in order to have more clarity in the translation.

Possibly the ultimate challenge (and pleasure) in translating Hebrew is the richness of biblical and liturgical allusions coded into the language itself.

In the title of "Grace After Meals" (ברכת המזון) there was a ready English equivalent. In "Post Partum II" however, the word "rechem" (רחם) literally means both "mercy" and "womb." In the translation, we had to skip the play on words and use two different phrases.

Sometimes I decided to reverse this process and take advantage of the thin membrane between the spiritual and the mundane. The English titles for both "Nativity" and "Litany" were chosen for their liturgical echoes. "Nativity" (מולד) could be translated as "birth," but the poem itself plays off a larger biblical story. The Hebrew title for "Litany" (התנצלות) actually means "apology" yet I felt that the poem read as a prayer and wanted a title that invoked that.

As in any project of this scope, one doesn't work alone. I owe a debt to those who helped explain and illuminate along the way. My brother, David Siegel, whose knowledge of Jewish texts was invaluable. My daughter, Nina Tokayer, who is herself a songwriter and has an ear for the melody beneath the words. My translator idols, Joanna Chen and Marcela Sulak, who cheered me on. Maya Tevet Dayan, who labored alongside me. And most importantly, Sarah Wetzel and the editors of Saturnalia Books, for their faith in these poems and their commitment to share them with the English-speaking world.

Jane Medved

I. Summer

JESUS

In the moonlight, by the Sea of Galilee
we consumed tall mountains
of fried egg and bread.

The women we called *Grandma*
were fifty years old.
The trunks of the palm trees sweated
even in the dark. The water
tasted like sugar and cinnamon.

Our hands were twelve years old.
Our legs were twelve years old.
All of our organs were twelve years old
and we had no idea they were even there.

In the dark, somebody said
they saw something over the water.
Someone else yelled *It's Jesus!*

We sat and chewed and watched.
The world was ancient,
stretching down into unfathomable darkness.
And we were so fresh.
Like a moonbeam on the water.
Like a miracle.

Cotton

When I imagine my childhood
as perfect, I remember you
and me, on a stack of cotton in the kibbutz,
small and raised up like two cherries
on top a mountain of whipped cream.

I conceal the swarm of bees
and my fear of them, the persistent
humming that saws towards us,
the sweat dripping down our backs,
the weight of the heat on our eyelids,
the itch that climbs from our feet to our necks,
the asbestos walls of the cotton barn
closing in on us like a chimney.

I blur the fear of heights,
the worry that that we will suddenly stop breathing
from all the cotton fibers pressing the air
and because you don't always need a reason
to stop breathing.

I erase everything I didn't know
then, everything that happened to you

on quiet nights without bees,
outside of this whiteness,
when you weren't on a soft peak,
and not in daylight,
and not with me, and not alone,
the windows of your body broken
wide open with night.
All those terrible nights.

There remains only our legs burrowing
into the whitest fluff,
our skinny knees, bones stretching
under the skin, far

from any portion of darkness.
We float above an abyss of silence,
bits of cotton in our hair. You smile—
your two front teeth leaning on each other
like the slats of a broken fence.

Leafing Through the Album

Here I am, and that girl, Shirley.
Turns out I didn't imagine her.
Her father still hasn't
hung himself from the bathroom ceiling
and she still hasn't
found him dangling like a dead curtain.
She is smiling at the camera in a short skirt
and white stockings. She is hugging
me, and I, her. Soon
in one moment, her father will give me
four baby chicks from the coop.
Four chicks!
It's still possible to imagine them growing
into roosters. The dog still hasn't
torn them apart in the dead of night.
The lawn is yellowing with the end of summer,
the wall of the coop behind us is stained with mud.
Time stretches out its long arms and dozes.

COME

Once I believed that time was an object
that could be thrown away
together with loneliness, that I could
toss out all those years

where there wasn't even one girl
who wanted to play with me in the afternoon.
I lay on the bed in my room and counted the minutes
until childhood would end.

And when it did, I threw that bed out.
I left home. I moved in with a guy.
I cut my hair short. I studied the nakedness
of my body through the hands of another. I ate
voraciously. I danced all night and slept all day.

As contrary as possible, as different
as different could be, I extricated myself
from the elevator of childhood
through a narrow crack of opportunity,
its doors almost shutting me in.

In the middle of this, I also left behind
my mother, forty-six years old,
still menstruating, still falling in love,
her long hair gathered in a sloppy hair pin,
making family dinners—

for everyone their favorite omelet
except for me, whose chair was always empty.
I only visited on weekends, to tell them about my nights.
I treated my father and her as day-people.
How she tried to understand me, to find out
what I was eating, how I spent my time.

Her questions rang bells of danger in my head,
those elevator doors gaping open like a maw.
I wouldn't even celebrate my birthday with her.

Nineteen years old, in lipstick and high heels,
childhood was so close I could hear it crashing
like a hungry ocean on the breakwater
heading back for me.

I walked into my childhood room, careful
not to look into the mirror.
The dress was spread out on the bed,
black, brand new, without gift wrap or ribbon,
thin as skin, as if just now emptied of a body

ready to be worn, like the clothes
my mother once laid out for me
every morning before we left for kindergarten,
hand in hand, sewn one to the other,
before we were split like a mourner's shirt.

In the note she had written—
Best of luck, my child
in whatever path you choose.
Years passed before those words reached me.
In that moment, shoving the dress into my backpack,
I am sure I read:
Come back. Be my child again.

MEMORIAL

We buried the bird
by our front gate, one wing stretched
to the right, the beak—to the left
as if she were flying
out of her body, in all directions,

her eyes wide open, like windows
in an empty house.
We tried to shut them, worried
about the sand getting in.

My little brother stood to one side
trying not to cry, meeting death
face to face for the first time, his bird

lying in the palms of our father
who bent over her
with the same apprehension
he used to cradle a raw fish,
before throwing it into the pan.

My mother suggested we say something,
perhaps sing.
We stood and listened to the quiet
the bird had left behind.

After all, she was a noisy bird,
she screeched day and night.
We even took her cage out
to the garden. We thought that being close
to nature would calm her down.

At night we covered her
with a blanket, which was both
necessary and illogical.

One day her wing feathers,
which had been clipped at the pet store,
grew back.
She escaped through a crack in the cage
and soared until she got stuck
on a nearby tree, paralyzed.

We had to lure her down
the trunk carefully. This bird
didn't know how to fly
nor how to live in captivity.

She never had a bird friend,
or any other friends.
As a speaking parrot, she only knew
one word and that too was distorted:
"Heddo! Heddo!"

What could we possibly say by her open grave—
That she died before her time?
That she lived life to the fullest?
No cliché worked in her case
other than to say that death released her
from her misery and us—

from our guilt.
I was young. I believed
that in the silence that gathered,
we'd hear the universe
telling us something.

That was the first time
I fell into this trap.

Rehabilitation

My father had one arm
barely hanging from his shoulder.
A piece of shrapnel had left a crater
there, deep as a bite from an apple.

Others had plastic legs
attached with straps, metal hooks
instead of fingers and glass eyes
gaping open in surprise, as pretty

as my marble collection.
I loved to examine them
on the grass by the edge of the pool
when they released the straps,
arms and legs left behind,
as they limped into the water
and swam stripped of their form—

I held a secret competition between them—
how many limbs can you take apart
and still remain a person?

The country's heroes; their pupils
sown with gun powder, foggy smiles
and faraway battle fields. In this place
they were a mathematical equation:
Twenty percent

disability was the entrance requirement
for this fabulous sports center.
My father had twenty-one percent—
like the weight in grams of a soul,
like the age at which he lost his friends.

The spirit of the Lord hovers over the face of the waters
and the waters are a rehabilitation pool. From here one doesn't
go forth to war. The war comes after you
hungry, tearing apart memories,
dreams, nights

full of dread. We went with him every Saturday,
my father's handicapped card a sparkling
sky blue, attached with a safety pin to his bathing suit.
We ate "Little Missile" sundae cones and played
on the firing range, eliminating entire people

made out of cardboard. Once, upon hearing a round
of bullets, one of the men burst into tears.
My father laid his jagged arm
on his shoulder. The man said,

I don't know why I'm crying—
about what was, about what is,
or about what is yet to come.

WE RETURN FROM THE SEA

Our feet were stained with tar. The world
was yellow and its edges burnt.
The sky, the earth and the air were an ear
and we had so much to tell.
At home, my mother's skin was still warm
and smelled sweet from coconut, from the sun,
from the water and from being alive.

The tar disappeared. The stains disappeared. The memory
of the stains. We didn't even notice. The sky
straightened out its edges and grew white.
Life spread out flat and wide.
We are left with feet that are always clean
and never say a thing.

HOME

What was that smell
that lingered in the rooms?
The haze of patties frying
in the kitchen, freshly
washed sheets stretched
out on metal beds, rain
against the window, the dust
of words sweet as talc,
and on the neck of the shirts
blossomed a scent that once
was a rose and before that
earth and rain, the lust between
sun and life.

I sat on the knees of others.
Their bellies held my back.
Their arms were my walls.
I had a home made out of people.

HIDING

I want to write about that door,
the front door I opened with the hands
of an eight-year-old, a fifteen-year-old,
a twenty-year-old, a forty-year-old.
I want to tell how I hid from my mother
one Friday afternoon, when I came home
from school, still wearing my backpack.
I stood outside the door for hours
and spied on her, watching how she waited
for me to arrive: her beautiful cheeks sinking
into themselves like parachutes emptied
of air, her eyes shooting their green arrows
in every direction without hitting a thing.

She wandered between the kitchen and living room
like a pendulum, lifting then replacing
the telephone, moving her lips like a silent film star.
I didn't hear a thing through the door.
How long did I stand and watch her like that?
Until she turned grey before my eyes?
Until the evening grew dark?
Perhaps I got cold. Perhaps I had pity on her,
a door of mercy opening inside me.

My mother almost fainted in my arms,
her eyes looking towards me
as if through a hollow tunnel that had at its end
the unimaginable, the unthinkable,
that which must now be erased from her memory.
I saved her
from the gaping abyss, from the capriciousness

of life, from my disappearance
and from her own disappearance.
For the first time in my life
I felt the responsibility of being loved
and it broke my heart.

At the Edge of the World

All summer long, hapless insects
crashed into our windows.
And in the fall they hung
like strings from the sill,
caught up in dust,
thin black sketches of death.

We asked questions without answers:
Are the souls of all creatures
the same size? Where do we go
from here? And what gives
birth to the rain?

Drops fell down every morning.
Once they were clouds and before that
an ocean in whose shallow waters
we stepped barefoot in summer.
And the waters were calm,
like clouds, like rain, like the imprint
of insects on a windowsill.

בקצה העולם

כָּל הַקַּיִץ הִתְעוֹפְפוּ חֲרָקִים עִם רַגְלַיִם
אֲרֻכּוֹת כְּחוּטִים, הִתְנַגְּשׁוּ בַּחַלּוֹנוֹת. וּבַסְתָו
הוּטְלוּ עַל אֶדֶן הַחַלּוֹן
מְסֻבָּכִים בְּאָבָק;
רְשׁוּמִים דַּקִּים וּשְׁחֹרִים שֶׁל מָוֶת.

שָׁאַלְנוּ שְׁאֵלוֹת שֶׁאֵין עֲלֵיהֶן
תְּשׁוּבָה: הַאִם לַחֲרָקִים דַּקִּים נְשָׁמוֹת
גְּדוֹלוֹת כְּמוֹ לְפִילִים? לְאָן כֻּלָּנוּ
מַמְשִׁיכִים מִכָּאן? וּמָה נִמְצָא
מֵעַל לַגֶּשֶׁם?

טִפּוֹת טִפְטְפוּ מֵעָלֵינוּ מִדֵּי בֹּקֶר. פַּעַם
הֵן הָיוּ עֲנָנִים, וְלִפְנֵי כֵן אוֹקְיָנוֹס
שֶׁבַּקַּיִץ פָּסַעְנוּ בְּמֵימָיו הָרְדוּדִים
בְּרַגְלַיִם יְחֵפוֹת. וְהַמַּיִם הָיוּ שְׁקֵטִים.
כְּמוֹ עֲנָנִים, כְּמוֹ גֶּשֶׁם
כְּמוֹ רְשׁוּמֵי חֲרָקִים עַל אֶדֶן חַלּוֹן.

II. Autumn

NATIVITY

Soon winter will return, and we will go out to the rain forest
that will never be ours, where small Christmas lights
outline pine trees against a foreign sky.
Darkness will fall at three-thirty in the afternoon, and at home
we'll mix hot cocoa in dark mugs.
The evening will draw out like a melody, and there will be plenty of time
to read poems and listen to the rain.
There will be leisure to discuss the future, to speak slowly and deliberately
as if it was under our control
and ignore the past which orphans us unceasingly.
As if sadness had never planted us here.
As if we had only just emerged
this very instant,
immaculate and wondering.

LITANY

The wind came down from the mountains that night
roaring like a highway,
or tall waves in the sea.
I heard in it strange words
of love, yearnings that passed over us
from a faraway place, afternoon sighs, unmade
beds and the murmuring of other children
whirling into one great noise.

And in the morning I couldn't stop
apologizing: I'm sorry
the dog barked. Forgive me,
that I can't find my place.

I asked to be saved together with you,
to eat by the table in the afternoon light.
The walls of our house wrapped around us like skin.

HOUSEKEEPING

I chase around with objects in my hands,
items out of place, always short
on time. I am a vast train station
and my hands are the many platforms.
To which destination will these socks be sent,
these notebooks, these pages, these dreams of words I wrote?

At times, I am an object moved
from place to place.
At times I am the Grand sorter.

For this I must be grateful:
This house released me
from my previous house,
just as this man released me
from my previous man.

Perhaps it is so with this life
and my previous lives.
Every time it gets too crowded,
I leave.

Autumn

Naked trees
net the sky above us,
touching each other with countless
fingers. Once we were like them.

I think of all the clothes
we've put on since then. So many
layers, all that terrible effort,

when one proper shedding is all we really need.

NOTES FROM THE JOURNEY

We are watching the sky
to differentiate between clouds
made by God
and the ones men have caused.
We hold our breath.
We left a land that abandoned us.
Our hearts yearn for ground
to build a home, plant a tree.
Our legs want to distance us
from what was left behind:
fear of war and grief,
that has nothing to do with war.
Our memories are our only possessions.
We sift through them like collectors,
sorting, giving them names.

Of what we once knew, little is left:
Words have the power to open and close.
Life and death are in the hands of language,
and language is held by the heart.
The keys to the heart work just like a car.
In order to love you don't need a passenger,
you just need to ignite.

A Leap of Imagination

I am sitting in this house
as the northern light filters
through the windows.
Loss has made me so insubstantial
that I can hear the trembling
of mountains shifting. I can place
love on two leaves of a scale
and know which is the heaviest.
Opposite me a treetop sways
against the window, and my heart
wanders towards it. The wind howls
outside – the trunk reaches
with its branches and I reach
with my arms. Apparently not much
is needed to become a tree,
and for the tree to become me.
Many women before me have turned
into saplings and rocks, straw is spun
into gold, peaks into clouds. The word of God
became the universe, destruction,
and then forgiveness. It shouldn't be that hard
for the two of us to be united again.

REDEMPTION WITH THE FALL OF EVENING

I skip above the land mines
of my life; a pickle on the carpet,
a piece of banana in the corner of the room,
crumbs of chalk; the girl
is at an age where she tosses everything.

I have calculated: ten times an hour,
one hundred times a day, two thousand
and eight hundred times to bend down
a month. And in objects: fifteen thousand
items that need to be put back in place.
I read once that lower back pain

is caused by financial worries.
That must have been written by a man.
Just like the story of Creation, and the rest of the Torah.
In my bible, God rises from the sink
in the evening, when the kitchen is clean.
Lavender and lemon scented angels
roll out the carpet of night beneath my legs
and a field of pure granite countertop
awaits to be sown with thoughts
there was no time for until now.

I vacuum up the leftovers of the big bang
of the day. Creation takes place to the sound of methodic
breathing from all the rooms. Nothing behind me,
nothing in front of me, even history
is still distant
in the future horizon of morning.

Every evening I am the first woman
on the same red couch in the living room,
created again in my old image.

FREEDOM

Here I am, a woman who escaped
from her house, hair a mess, putting on lipstick
I found in the car, wearing yesterday's sweater,
and behind me:

crying babies, a half cooked pot of rice,
a to-do list that will never be completed,

gloves and shoes tossed into the hall,
an avalanche with no rescue in sight.

Someone will probably trip on that mess
and I won't be there to pick up the pieces.

By virtue of the good karma
I have accumulated in previous lives,
and by virtue of a feminism
that ran out of speed halfway to its mark,
here I am—

with the right to vote, to choose, to be chosen,
to love, to earn a living, to get a job,
celebrating
the two hours of my independence
in the coffee shop closest to my home.

Me and my sweeping ban on gluten,
on dairy, my stomach pains,
all that was lost and all that remains

from the last birth, the aching back,
and the sweet forgetting
of what actually being awake feels like,
lifting up my chin, despite it all,
for two working hours in this coffee shop.

The air of freedom smells like pie,
the coffee comes only with milk,
and the chairs are perfect for women
who have never given birth, for people
without a womb, and for all those
whose pelvic floor still functions.

The long chain of women before me
resting in heaven—holding
onto embroidery threads, the best of world
literature and homemade dried fruits—
are applauding me with invisible hands,
cheering on my laptop,
which opens in a storm.

My grandmother, who refused to go to the mikveh.
My great grandmother who read books in secret.
Her mother's mother, who had four Russian horses.
They took along with them to a better world, their backbone.

I say to them—
I am the sum of my unfinished tasks.

The deadline closes in on me.
The socks are scattered, and I still haven't cooked,
haven't submitted,
haven't cleaned up,
haven't sent anything.

They cheer for me, those fools.
For them, lack of leisure
is a sign of success.

AUSTRALIA

I'm telling you about everything I managed
to get done when you weren't home—
I planted basil in the garden, as two pots
simmered on the kitchen stove, all the while
the baby in my arms. How long will we continue
with these heroic stories? Perhaps you remember
where we put the horizon?

I haven't seen it for a while. The most beautiful,
sunny day of the year, I spent in the Supermarket
chasing the girls with my eyes
as they ran down the aisles, and wondering
about our membership card, which had suddenly,
for no apparent reason, stopped collecting points.

Perhaps I'll never know another summer
like the one when I circled all of Australia
in an old Subaru station wagon,
a tent and two boxes in the trunk,
one for vegetables, and one for fruit.
I shopped at farms. I stayed away
from crocodiles, all day in a skirt and bikini top,
the horizon was spread so far and wide
it actually seemed like the outline of the universe.

.

How did I leave Australia? Wide open
as the door to a house, when you step out
for a moment to the garden, careless and free.
I promised myself I'd come back.

Everything I dreamt for back then, in single beds,
was about this family, this check-out line in the market,
this membership card, grated yellow cheese
sold by the pound, blades of grass
stuck to the clothes at the end of the day.

I never imagined that I would wander here
and remember those other vast skies,
a red desert, earth just like this, but different.

MARRIED LIFE

By day we swap places
with each other, rushing
like workers
on a factory floor

assembling a life:
meals, dishes, carpool.
The door opens and shuts,

as the house inhales
then exhales us,
inwards, outwards.

Our words gather
above us, dark as clouds
hanging from the ceiling,
close to bursting.

Peaks of laundry encircle
as we separate
colors from white, insult
from anger, memories
from grudges, day from night.

Only in the dark, can the hungry
mouths of our skin
gape open—the largest digestive
system of the body.

We feed each other, like cannibals,
living flesh in sweet revenge:
an eye for an eye,
a limb for a limb,
heart beating heart.

The best of ourselves we save
for the end of the day,

like a note on the margins
that sheds its light onto everything.

EXTINCTION

On the day of our eleventh wedding anniversary
the last white rhino in the world died.
In retrospect, it's good we didn't celebrate.
As it is, that day became impossible

to forget. A race was exterminated,
hunted down to grind from its horn, powder

that enhances virility. On the night of the wedding
my dress was zipped so tight, it took forever
to get it off, and the tear that spread through sheer stockings
accomplished in seconds
what the powder of a rhino's horn
achieved through massive deaths.
What does it do to the world

when a species disappears?
The African gamekeeper
bent over the rhinoceros, pressed a black forehead
to a white body
whose likeness will never be born again, will never die,
the last remnant of an ancient world
in which it was enough to have thick skin and a horn
in order to survive, where the rhino was large and man small,

man and woman joined together in order
to plant inside their bodies
a wild and savage history. Now

only one thing is clear; the world is fragile and incomplete,
like lace that has suddenly torn a thread,

a hole widening in the shape of a rhino, imperceptible
as the point of a needle in stockings;

you see how it begins,
you understand where it is going,
you know it can't be stopped.

ALTERNATE LIFE

In my alternate life
I am that young girl opposite me
on the ferry deck, wrapped in a blue coat.
The fur on the brim of my hat hides my eyes.
The boy who came out on the deck with me
is trying to light his cigarette in the wind.
In my alternative life this is me
edging closer to him now, one warm breath away,
cupping the flame that flares and dies out,
guarding it from the wind with two fearless hands.
It's the beginning of November, but I'm not cold.
Hot blood erupts in my body like a geyser,
rises through my long, strong legs
to my head, flung from the earth's lava, boiling.

The boy sends me a look. His smile
is now an offering for me alone,
private, secret, like a crack
of possibility. The edges of his hat
touch the fur of my coat.
Between us the cigarette burns.

ALTERNATE LIFE
חיים חלופיים

בַּחַיִּים הַחֲלוּפִיִּים שֶׁלִּי
אֲנִי הַבַּחוּרָה הַזֹּאת מוּלִי
עֲטוּפָה בְּמְעִיל כָּחֹל עַל סִפּוּן הַמַּעְבֹּרֶת.
הַפַּרְוָה בְּשׁוּלֵי הַכּוֹבַע מַסְתִּירָה לִי אֶת הָעֵינַיִם.
הַבָּחוּר שֶׁיָּצָא אִתִּי לַסִּפּוּן
מְנַסֶּה לְהַדְלִיק לְעַצְמוֹ סִיגַרְיָה בָּרוּחַ.
בַּחַיִּים הַחֲלוּפִיִּים זוֹ אֲנִי
מִתְקָרֶבֶת אֵלָיו עַכְשָׁו, בְּמֶרְחָק נְשִׁימָה חַמָּה מִמֶּנּוּ,
חוֹפֶנֶת אֶת הָאֵשׁ שֶׁשָּׁבָה וְנִכְבֵּית, מְגִנָּה עָלֶיהָ
בְּחֵרוּף יָדַיִם חֲשׂוּפוֹת מִפְּנֵי הָרוּחַ.
לֹא קַר לִי בִּתְחִלַּת נוֹבֶמְבֶּר
עַל הַסִּפּוּן. דָּם חַם מִתְפָּרֵץ בַּגּוּף
כְּמוֹ גֵּיזֶר, עוֹלֶה מֵהָרַגְלַיִם הַחֲזָקוֹת וְהָאֲרֻכּוֹת שֶׁלִּי
עַד הָרֹאשׁ, מִסְתַּעֵר מִתּוֹךְ הַלַּבָּה שֶׁל הָעוֹלָם, רוֹתֵחַ.

הַבָּחוּר מֵרִים אֵלַי מַבָּט. הַחִיּוּךְ שֶׁלּוֹ
מֻגָּשׁ עַכְשָׁו רַק לִי,
פְּרָטִי, סוֹדִי, כְּמוֹ סֶדֶק
שֶׁל אֶפְשָׁרוּת. שׁוּלֵי הַכּוֹבַע שֶׁלּוֹ נוֹגְעִים
בְּפַרְוַת הַמְּעִיל שֶׁלִּי.
בֵּינֵינוּ הַסִּיגַרְיָה בּוֹעֶרֶת.

III. WINTER

It's January Again. What Would I Be Telling You Now?

For two months the snow rested above us,
and when it melted, we discovered
that everything underneath was still alive.
The cabbages even more purple.

*

Abigail made me breakfast:
almonds, yellow cheese,
dates. I tell you, from year to year
the small gifts multiply.

*

From the odd socks without a partner,
Naomi-li and I fashion bunny dolls.
She tells me: *In school they call this
 "Recycling"*
I talk to her about the cycle of rebirth.

*

At night, on the rocking chair in the living room,
Elinor is small in my arms, and in her arms
I am huge,
as we wait on the platform
for the train of sleep.

*

In the afternoon—soft bread,
orange juice, the maple tree in the window.
Silence seeps in hidden ways
from the clouds into the skin.

*

I ask: Have you seen our new checkered tablecloth?
Our Friday Night Sabbath meals?
The forests that climb up the mountainside?
You answer me: My sweet girl,

*

the whole world is a bridge,
and the bridge is made out of ropes,
and the ropes are umbilical cords
that are never disconnected.

*

It is four years since you died.
Where do I begin?

EVERGREEN

A.

The path takes me to the forest, to a small town called *Evergreen*, named after the greenery and after eternity, and not for a king, a politician or a writer. I sleep in a hut between the trees, awaken among the trees, cook alongside them, inhale the air they emit at night. By the fireplace, my hostess whispers a secret: once a woman turned into a tree. I reveal to her: once a woman lived in a city on a street named after another city. Suddenly I don't remember if I ever chose to live in the city. If I even knew it was possible to do otherwise. I am forty-one years old, and not sure of anything anymore.

B.

At night I walk into the forest alone. The quiet is vast, wider than the silence of the kibbutz at night, deeper than the silence of the desert. Once upon a time there was a woman who turned into a tree, who sent out roots into the layers of silence, near the heart of the world. Wolves walked past her, tigers, antelope, and never realized that she was a woman. Thoughts crossed over her face and moved on, the sound of words floated by, memories. Perhaps her daughter also passed her in the dark, her footsteps making a lone sound. *If a bear comes he'll devour me in silence.* I am not frightened by this thought.

A still death in the dark forest, suddenly seems like a beautiful event.

C.

A year before her death, my mother went to a medical center in the Black Forest. For six weeks she drank juices, stepped into the forest for the first time, slept in the forest and asked to save her life. When she returned, she wasn't any healthier. The doctor was angry with her, for wasting time and for her naiveté. My mother sat there blushing, her green eyes flickering like leaves in the sunshine. The doctor's words went past her like the buzz of a fly. My mother was in love. *This is the way to live*, she told me. I was beside myself with worry. But mostly, I was happy, that even in her illness, she managed to find this kind of joy.

Once upon a time there was a mother who asked for a forest. Four years after her death, I understand.

D.

The trees speak between themselves, through their crowns and their roots, connected in the sky and beneath the earth. I am only familiar with relationships between people: fractures, disagreements, and misunderstandings, streets that cut into each other, corners with straight edges. After my mother's death, I signed up for a course in parapsychology, desperate to speak with her again. On the first day, the teacher sent us to talk to the trees, to question them and listen to their response. Someone asked, *How do I know the answer I'm receiving is really coming from the tree? That I'm not making it up?* The teacher answered – you will just know.

E.

One night, a tree speaks to me. Its trunk is thick and yellowed, its branches rich with leaves, dense as a cloud, rustling like rain, even in the dark, still air. It speaks clearly and distinctly. *Find your crown*, it tells me. *Find your root system.* I know about roots. I have been searching for them most of my life. I never thought in terms of a treetop. My glance goes upwards, to the place where the edges of this tree meet the edges of the other trees, blessed with a kiss of sky. I go to sleep with this new thought of crown and foliage. In the morning, in the light, I discover that someone has carved a face into its bark.

My Mother Invites a Doctor for Lunch

He arrives at five after twelve
during the afternoon break from the clinic,
lowering his head

in order not to hit the door frame.
The hair on the top of his head is thinning
like oxygen at the peak of a mountain.

My mother seats him in my chair,
dressed in her pastel sweater,
thrilled that he agreed to come.
She believes in co-existence

with physicians.
The yellow winter light enters
through the geranium pot on the window
and pours onto our backpacks
strewn around the kitchen floor,
the doctor glances down

to the painted tiles
that my parents bought in Jaffa.
My mother says *Make yourself at home,*
and immediately there is the span

of a desert between us.
She serves chicken soup, asks if he
would also like carrots,
when is he planning to get married,
how did he decide to become a doctor,
how long does it take to get here
from the village every morning.
He sips the soup
without a sound. It would be possible
to imagine he's not even there,
if he wasn't as tall as the minaret of a mosque
in the middle of our dining room.

What did we know about Arabs?
That they murder women and children,
they shout, they water down gasoline,
sell horse meat, have arranged marriages,
that they have no idea what love is.

The Doctor says thank you and agrees
to another serving. My sister and I
watch his hand and how the spoon arrives
at his mouth precisely, lifting from the bowl
like an airplane taking off above
an ocean of boiling soup, being swallowed

in a different universe.
Under his heavy eyelashes stretches
the line of a far horizon, his gaze
looking through us. We are scared
to ask ourselves, what does he know about Jews?

Afterwards, he bends over again
drooping like a flower stem, on his way out.
My mother invites him to come back soon.
Of course, he says.
But he never does. He turns instead

to his own future –
the village, the wedding, the continuation
of his balding, the traffic jams, and his promotion
to director of the clinic,
and my mother turns to her future—

to live, become sick and die young
and in between—
pots empty and fill
like hearts,
and bowls follow the necessary path
of cupboard-table-sink-cupboard,
orbiting the kitchen
that has become our world.

I only saw him once more,
years later, when I stood at the entrance
to his office, trying to get a prescription
for my mother, that he wouldn't agree to give me.
He explained about the new regulations
as if he didn't know
what love was. I screamed at him.
What I wouldn't give for a happy ending.

I remember that moment clearly:
me and my crying and everything I knew about doctors
and mothers, slipping out of me
bubbling, boiled sadness.

THREE YEARS SINCE YOUR DEATH

The leaves of the maple tree in my garden
are red and damp from the rain.
I have stopped expecting to see the sun-
bathed nuts you loved between its branches.
I drive a car much larger than I need. The street
signs are written in the mother tongue of others.
Yellow traffic lights sway beneath their wires,
but there is no wind and no promise of wind.
I turn a key inside the lock of a house
built by strangers, for people who are not you,
and not me, in a time that proceeded both of us.
I know how to point out four kinds of wheat
in English, and to choose bread from a bakery
where there is not one thing from the ground
where you are buried, from where you bore me.
I have learned the movements of a frozen winter
vaster and stiller than the winter that held you
in its arms as you passed from your body.
Where did you go? Where did I go?

If we ran into each other in the street today
you would ask *Is that you?* And perhaps
I wouldn't know how to answer.

Rome

When the tests showed the tumor had reached the liver,
we rushed to buy tickets to Rome.
My mother asked. *Is it because of my situation? Is this a farewell trip?*
Of course not, we answered.
It's summertime, and when will the three of us

have the opportunity again?
We climbed the steep, narrow stairs
to our rented apartment.
My mother and sister stepping lightly,
and me, holding my stomach
at thirty-three weeks,
as my hemoglobin kept
dropping
       and dropping.

In plazas, in parks, at fountains, by the meat and cheese vendors,
in the night market, in claustrophobic alleyways
whose walls were the mustard color
of hepatitis, my mother
and sister floated, and I
dragged
      the heavy
          weight

of my legs. In Rome a waiter called us
Cheap Jews. My mother bought
a ring. We rented a three-seated bicycle
we didn't manage to peddle. We were overcome
by my weakness
and excess weight. In Rome we turned

the hourglass over.
The first grains dropped
into the vacuum of our future
but we heard them loud and clear

echoing in the stone streets
heavy as drums
announcing the end.

THE RIGHT VERSION

Our time runs out in front of us
shrinking like light in the margins of the day,
but we insist on counting backwards
in accumulating years, the silver anniversaries,
and the gold, the births, the strength, the innocence,
to prop up thick biographies
padded with lists of descendants and possessions,

like a person leaving for a long journey
who doesn't look at the horizon spread in front of him,
but measures with his eyes over his shoulder
the growing distance
with every step from home.

Maybe it's better to tell the story of our lives
in short sentences,
in the shrinking hours of sleep,
in small wandering bites.

To begin with God.
To end with one last grain of sand.

TIDES

My daughter asked to sleep on the sofa
tonight. I say I understand, even though
I don't. I sit next to her
in the wilderness of a dark living room,
a mother and daughter in some prehistoric
time, exposed outside of the rooms.

This is what I understand about the world—
when the moon is full, the ocean
rises to its rim, and when the moon empties,
the water recedes and the heart is diminished.

Through the long chain of births,
through all the women who bore, and then protected
one another, this fear has now been passed
down to me, the fear that must never be named
rippling in the dark.

We are in the living room, under the empty moon,
abandoned. The child moves in her sleep.
The dog circles her kennel.
She's the only one I can calm down.

SMOKE

All night long we heard steps on the roof.
In the morning we discovered a skunk had sprayed the dog.
The neighbor looked at her, said *you poor thing*,
and sent us to wash her in tomato juice.

Instead, we lit incense after incense on the path
in the yard, all the way
from her kennel to the house. We lived inside
sweet flowery smoke. Fragrant rot
from India burned in our Canadian back yard
and compressed our lives
into a cloud outside of time and place.

Four nights in a row we laughed. Almost happy.
Almost normal. We laughed until tears
came, and immediately used them
to cry. Whatever we had lost came back
with the smoke—

entire lives, up to the last dish and glance,
meals and wine glasses, words that were heard
and doors that enclosed fully furnished worlds.
The people who once lived with us,
whom we had lost,

transparent now, filling up the spaces
between us completely:
not bothered by the smell,
not bothered by the laughter,
not bothered by the dog's snout
black and wet, pressed
against the crack in the door.

THE SILENCE AFTER

What are the winter storms here
compared to the deluge I have passed through?
I walk in the rain without blinking,
and gaze through it quietly
at the leaves that are flushed from the cold.
What is their redness compared to the blood
I have seen? I gathered the avalanche
of my mother's body in my arms.
I pulled the strings of her breath against
the direction of the wind. I entered the fire.
I was blinded in the eye of the storm.

Now, all this is behind me.
I roast potatoes in the oven once again.
I sprout seeds in jars.
I listen to the tidings of the clouds.

GRACE AFTER MEALS

My father stands over the pots
in my house, baking sweet potatoes,
giving me back the taste
of a world where mothers still exist.

His hands slice thin answers
to my questions, laying
them in orderly rows: consequences,
actions, reasons, reactions.

We learn the hard way. This is a world
of the eaters and the eaten: sadness consumes
the heart, and we consume the sadness.
In large spoonfuls, quickly, with coarse salt
and a delicate heart. We no longer linger
around the table, least it swallow us whole.

Blessed be the one who brings forth bread,
who sustains his world
with beauty, grace and sorrow.
Blessed be the creator of my father.

HUNGER

In the middle of the night I get hungry.
As morning breaks in my faraway country
I spoon yogurt into a cup,
grab two cherry tomatoes by the hand,
eat and stare at the snowy darkness.

My mother also foraged in the fridge
every night, driven by a confusion of body
and hunger, the pot lids rejoicing
like cymbals. As did her mother and her grandmother.
Generations of nocturnal predators.

But now I eat
like trees that have been planted far from their native land
and blossom twice: once in the new spring
and once in the spring they came from—

rooted in two soils,
awake and dreaming at the same time,
welcoming every night the face
of a morning that has yet to rise.

Alone on the Bright Mountain

We fell in love in a warm country.
We said things like "soft as snow,"
without ever seeing
snow, and we learned to identify
the smallest birds
by long and ponderous names.

But here, alone on the bright mountain,
one can actually say "soundless as snow"
and allow the birds to float away
like the soul in its moment of wonder.

Before we broke up, you said to me—
Don't worry, even a lifetime of silence is temporary,
like life itself, and all that comes afterwards.

And since then, we are as quiet
as the frozen clearing of a forest,
waiting for one beam of sunlight.

On top of this bright mountain
I am thinking, perhaps
words are what happens
to silence when it melts.

She-Bear

In my winter slumber, I dream
of you. Another way to pass the hard season.
The tempo of my heartbeat slows,
the rhythm of my breath is missing,
and I don't go out again to hunt in the snow
for who we never were.

My body is almost frozen.
My mouth doesn't demand a thing.
Silence flickers like a flame,
illuminating the drawings on the cave of my heart.

POSSIBILITY

Imagine I am resting my head
upon your knees, lying on the living
room carpet, while above us
the sounds of the *oud* fly like doves.
Your fingers in my hair, the scent of your clothes
in my breath, the beating warmth,
your chest beneath my car.
I would speak and you would answer,
one outline enclosing the two of us.

Imagine I had stayed.

The Law of Conservation of Matter

The darkness falls now at three o'clock,
and instead of making lunch
we gather at home, to hug each other
and sleep. Somewhere else in the world
light pours like a waterfall,
people's eyes squint, and their mouths
curve into a dazzling smile.

Nothing in the world disappears.
Snow melts into rivers,
rivers carry memories,
and the memories, in their time, freeze over
to return and melt.
Eyes that we have already forgotten
live on inside us, green and sprouting.

The sorrows of separation shift
like continents: from heart to belly and beyond that.
The body changes like a landscape.

I think about the baby
my mother bore, before
she gave birth to me.
We never knew if she died or disappeared.

Where has she gone? Where have I?

WHEREVER WE FLOAT

My daughter rests her head on my stomach
as if listening to a large conch shell.
She hears inside me the murmur of ancient winds
and looks for clues.
Not long ago, she left this stomach
cast out by the waves.

Now I am the giant raft
and my daughter sleeps on me.
I am the turtle upon which the universe is placed,
and the universe is my daughter.
I am the great body, substance and bones,
and my daughter carries a thousand dreams.

Beneath us and around us
is an ocean made of love
and the soft glow from the hallway
is a lighthouse.

Wherever we float,
that's home.

WHEREVER WE FLOAT

לאן שנצוף

בִּתִּי מַנִּיחָה אֶת רֹאשָׁהּ עַל בִּטְנִי
כְּמַאֲזִינָה לְצֶדֶף גָּדוֹל,
שׁוֹמַעַת בִּי רַחַשׁ רוּחוֹת עַתִּיקוֹת
וְקוֹרֵאת רְמָזִים
לֹא מִזְּמַן יָצְאָה מַהַבֶּטֶן הַזֹּאת,
נִפְלֶטֶת מִתּוֹךְ הַגַּלִּים.

עַכְשָׁו אֲנִי הַמָּצוֹף הָעֲנָק
וּבִתִּי יְשֵׁנָה עָלַי
אֲנִי הַצָּב, שֶׁעָלָיו מֻנָּח הַיְקוּם
וְהַיְקוּם הוּא בִּתִּי
אֲנִי הַגּוּף הַגָּדוֹל, חֹמֶר וַעֲצָמוֹת
וּבִתִּי נוֹשֵׂאת רִבּוֹא חֲלוֹמוֹת.

מִתַּחְתֵּינוּ וּמִסְּבִיבֵנוּ
אוֹקְיָנוֹס מֵימֵי הָאַהֲבָה
וְאוֹר קָטָן בַּמִּסְדְּרוֹן מִחוּץ לַחֶדֶר
הוּא מִגְדַּלּוֹר.

לְאָן שֶׁנָּצוּף שָׁם בַּיִת.

IV. Spring

OTHER PEOPLE'S HOUSES

A.

For weeks we've been living in other people's houses. I open the door,
turn on the light, peek inside suspiciously. The girls race past me. In less
than a minute they have decided where everyone will sleep, they know the
location of all the games, and which secret door leads to the yard with the
hammock in it. I want to be like them, to throw myself into the world as if
it were a warm bath. Too many layers of life have made me suspicious. I
squint my eyes, check if the floor is clean enough to take off our shoes.

Instead of being like my daughters, I have become my mother.

B.

Once, in a hotel in London, we switched rooms three times. My mother
kept finding—ants in the bathtub, stains on the sheets, dust in the cur-
tains—I dragged after her with the suitcases from room to room. I was
eighteen years old and I told her I didn't understand her at all.

C.

Afterwards I lived in the kind of homes my mother didn't understand. In
fact, other than the apartment near Sheinken street, she couldn't fathom any
house I chose. When I moved in with a bearded guy to a trailer in the fields,
she wouldn't set foot inside.

D.

She died shortly after I got married, after I had children, after she washed the floors of my house, music in the background, dancing with the mop. In one fell swoop, everyplace was emptied of her. She left me homeless, belonging simultaneously to everywhere and nowhere.

Except, like equanimity, that's not a solution that actually exists.

E.

For weeks already we are living in other people's houses. When my dead mother and I finish checking the towels, the sink, the ants, we try to sniff out who lives in this house. From time to time, my mother asks, *Who leaves their house like this for strangers? It's obvious that they will snoop around.* In her opinion it's never for the money. It's about people's need to expose themselves to others.

Even if they are not in front of them.

F.

We lived in a wooden hut on the shores of a lake in California, that belonged to a widow who had moved on to be with her new love. I took from her the name of the laundry detergent she used, and her courage to reinvent herself.

We lived on the border of Oregon, in the colorful house of an anthroposophist artist, and child with behavioral problems. At night I stayed awake to read the books on her bedroom shelf. I pretended that I grew up and belonged there.

We lived on a farm, with two shaggy horses outside the door, and in a small apartment in San Francisco, with an automatic light in the pantry and a view of the city from the window. In both places I vowed to myself, this is the only way to live, but I didn't stay.

G.

We lived in the forest, in a circular house. In the middle of the ceiling, instead of a light, they put a window. The sky trickled down through it. When I lay underneath, jealousy crept into my heart, of the sky, whose name in Hebrew—*shamayim*

is always in the plural.

METAMORPHOSIS

Right arm lifted to the ceiling,
left sideways, chin to the sky

facing the television in the living room, my love
duplicates with miraculous effort
the movements of the Flag Bearers in the ceremony
for Israel's Independence Day.
His back is turned away from the window, the maple tree,
the morning, and all of this Canada.

The Star of David rises from the transparent flag in his hand,
hovering over the room like a liberated butterfly.

It seems he has completely recovered
from the events of yesterday: The Inuit neighbor
got cut and my love touched a drop of blood
on the floor. In the panicked frenzy that followed

he didn't know what to do with himself: What if the Inuit
was carrying AIDS? Contagious hepatitis?
Hidden Ebola? What if he just got back
from Mexico along with a dormant virus?

That night he emptied my perfume bottle
onto his finger, coughing up the smoky scent
of roses, studying the palm of his hand
like a diamond dealer examining an unpolished stone.

Skin is made out of opening upon opening,
what if two bloods had been mixed together?

In his mind he was already becoming wider, shorter,
his thighs rounding out, the growing span of his shoulders

stretching the muscles between artic poles.
Foreign blood cells, stealthy as hunters in the snow,
were making their way up his arm, infiltrating

his heart, thick furs, raw fish,
wild game speared on their daggers,
a living, breathing threat on the chosen nation

that is my love.

At night he was afraid to fall asleep.
How will he recognize himself in the morning
through the procession of narrow canoes
that are now his eyes?

We held hands in the dark, taking advantage
of the last recognizable moments,
sun-kissed memories
of army, wars and oranges.

I Want an Electric Juicer

Why electric? What's wrong with the real kind?
my dead grandmother asks. *All of our lives
we squeezed oranges by hand.*

Why should she work so hard if there's an easier way?
That's my mother, from her life in the beyond.

You two are always looking to spend money,
my grandmother grumbles. An entire life and death,
and she's still lecturing us.

Buy yourself one and I'll pay for it, my mother ends the discussion
as if she still has a bank account
as if I am not paying from my pocket
for all the gifts she has bought me, since her death.

I'll buy it for you, Bubbaleh,
my grandmother concedes, lifting
the burden, as usual, from my mother.

After all, she has left us a goodly amount
from all the taxis she never rode,
the leftover food she refused to throw away,
the tea bag she dipped into the same cup until it fainted,
the socks she darned. What will I leave behind

except for tormented conversations with the dead?
What will I manage to put aside from all the coins
accumulated on my behalf, through endless hours of labor,
human lives, hard working generations. I don't even like

oranges. *But you need vitamin C for your health*, my dead
grandmother interjects. See, we are starting up again.

WHAT IS IMPORTANT IN LIFE

The neighbors all talked about two old women
who died a month apart, in the same building—
Safta Layka and her neighbor Rachel,
who always wrestled with the question
what was more important, to exercise or to clean
the house.

Rachel came down half a floor every day
and knocked on the door, as my grandmother slipped away
to her class at the country club, grumbling
Doesn't she have a life of her own?
But when she died suddenly, from cosmetic surgery,
my grandmother acquiesced to share a common fate:
Look what is happening to us. We're dying!

My grandmother prepared soup, strained it
of leaves, stems, vegetables and chicken, poured it
into empty cheese containers, and froze it.
Rachel's descendants sat in a polished, sparkling
clean house to mourn her. We mourned
my grandmother by eating the last batch
of her defrosted chicken soup.

EXILE

Houses that were once mine, are locked against me
forever. Now, I am an outsider
everywhere. Jars of preserves bring back to me
sugary days with my grandmother,
and closed shutters remind me of darkening
afternoons on metal beds that don't exist anymore.
Beyond the shades of strange windows
the mango voice of my grandfather slices
the distance into segments.
On doorways that were once mine
signs with strange names have been put up.
The faintest smell of frying patties
confuses my mind. I want to stretch out my arm,
open the door again.

KINNERET

Like a pin stuck into glass:
My grandfather in the water,
a fishing pole in hand.

The guilt of the camps sharpens
like a mirror. An arm waving good-bye
with a handkerchief, faces
that were left before their time
now
water.

There is no holocaust, no
weeping, no
creases.

Soon he will go inside, fill
my grandmother's sink
with fish,

his heart twitching between worlds.

AMERICA

Someone had drawn square fields,
a round ocean, narrow paths
to a low house and had placed us
inside of it, small and pale,
a grandmother and child.

The sun beat down. We wrote letters
on top of the plastic tablecloth in the kitchen.
The minutes of the afternoon gathered together
infinitesimal as grains of rice.

It's hot here (You spoke, I translated
into English) *We are all getting older.*
Soon my granddaughter will celebrate her Batmitzvah.
Tell us about yourselves.

Stanley broke his leg. (They answered. I read aloud)
Anne and Jim are away on vacation.
We're here, in California, always thinking about you.

The unwritten sentences grew between them
tied to me like an umbilical cord:
The memory of frozen plums in a Lithuanian cellar.
The kibbutz baking in a heat wave. America.

I was precise with the words. I believed
they would be enough to erase
wars, to heal a life that had been shattered.

I didn't understand time like you did.
I thought I could still turn the vessel of death onto its face.

EVIDENCE

I remember my grandmother
sucking on a chicken bone, cracking it with her teeth
to suckle the essence of the brown bone.
My grandmother also wore pearls,
put on make-up, danced a lot,
sometimes did laps in the pool, and toured
the world from the backs of elephants
and ships, and nevertheless
this is the image of her that sticks with me:
grabbing on to a *poulke* as if seizing a moment,
her babyish eyes half closed.

My mother would destroy any photograph
where she thought she didn't look pretty enough.
She eliminated with precision
any remnant that might remain after her,
examining every fingerprint
she had left behind in the world.
I remember her ripping up photos
of herself into small pieces like confetti,
a multicolored rain of memories erased,
one long celebration flowing from her palms,

swallowed into the forgetful abyss
of our kitchen garbage can.
On her face, the smile of a small victory
in the obliteration of evidence.

Responsibility

A photograph that my mother
wished to remember
hangs framed, in her home
and photos of her
hang in other houses, surrounded
by frames, and the people who wish
to remember her face.

Like ants who carry on their backs,
crumb by crumb of what was once
a loaf of bread,
our lives are too small to bear
the memory of all the generations.

Once, in a flea market in London,
we came across another family's photo album.
My mother flipped between the faces,
stalling over the smiling mustaches
and the dresses billowing with pride
behind upright sofas, and let slip
Who sells their own albums?

Nonetheless, from a sense of responsibility,
she bought a few photos from it.
They have joined the pictures we kept of her
in our family box of mementoes.

DEFROSTING

The frozen fish thaws and comes back to life.
We saw it in a video: Two people took it out of the freezer
and tossed it into a tub of water. For a moment it floats in circles
and then, a bubble appears, it flutters, twists, swims,
voices cheer in a foreign language.

We searched for a slight of hand, freezing
the picture on the screen:
this fish, fossilized, snowy,
like the fish in Savta Layka's freezer
that sometimes fell from the open door
onto our feet, sliding to the edge of the floor.

The fish from which she made Gefilte fish—
defrosted, cooked, chopped, mixed,
sweetened, molded patties with her hands
and then—placed them in the fridge, quivering
crowns of carrot on their heads,
new brides, plump and blind.

I couldn't bear this vision of resurrection.
They're probably Russian or Japanese, you said,
Who else would throw a frozen fish into a tub?
We laughed. We knew it was a distraction
from our own personal Ice Age

that we didn't know how to defrost;
experts in sorrow, in separation,
accepting the ways of the world,
always in mourning, never attempting
to resuscitate a thing.

GUARANTEE

I can still hear my mother's grandmother
saying goodbye after our weekly visit to her house.
Instead of parting in the usual manner,
she would lift up her hand, and yell out the window
the address of the house we had just left:
28 BODENHIEMER STREET!

Least we suddenly forget the number of her house,
or the name of her street. We wouldn't even remember
that we had forgotten. We would never see each other again.

She knew that forgetting is capricious,
time is opaque, and memory, like the heart,
fogs up. We laughed at her.
We believed in youth, in clarity.
We waved back at her with untroubled hands.

POST PARTUM (I)

Not a Goddess of Fertility.
Not the renewal of creation.
Not God speaking through my body.
Not the roar of past generations.

You extracted yourself from me
like a butterfly emerging from its cocoon,
like a snake shedding its old skin,
like peas that leave behind them
an empty shell.

POST PARTUM (II)

I am moving away from God.
My daughter has been born and God is repeating
the act of creation with other women in delivery rooms,
in bedrooms, in birthing pools and lakes.

I am left to mourn the tear
and the mending. And like an old woman
I tell anyone who agrees to listen
about the extraction—
this is how my body was emptied of my daughter.
This is how creation left me.

Against my will, and from my will
with a great cry, and in great abandonment.
We were one, strangers to each other
like a body and its internal organs.

I turn my prayer inwards
morning and evening,
in the fading afternoon and at rest.
My womb, have mercy on me, have mercy.

BABY GIRL

We are converging on you now:
wrinkled and beautiful, excited and bent
by destiny, ancient as crumbling papers
and fresh as a dream. The fragments
of our hearts, and our moments
of happiness, stretch from the dawn
of creation to the milky lashes of your eyes.

Your fathers, and your father's fathers, and their mother's mothers –
All of us crowd together at your entrance.

Just as the entire night wishes to compress
into one small star, we are now
your fingers, your nose, a cry, the twitch of a mouth.
We were many endings.
We grew very tired.
Now we begin again.

My Daughter is the Gateway to the Night

My daughter is the gateway to the other night.
Skies pour like dark, sweet milk.
Silky breaths drift into clouds.
An eyelid of moon appears above.
From the depth of the leaves, dreams are blown to us.
We are not awake. We are not asleep.

The sips of my daughter pulse
like a heart. At one end of this night: the dances
we spun in the evening. At the other end:
the stories we haven't told yet.

All around us, the transparent generations
of mothers and daughters who rose
and slept their lives between light and darkness,
from sleep to awakening to sleep,
they birthed one another and were forgotten.

My daughter is the gateway to the soft dawn
onto everything I was born
to remember once again.

My Daughter is the Gateway to the Night

בתי היא השער אל הלילה

בִּתִּי הִיא הַשַּׁעַר אֶל הַלַּיְלָה הָאַחֵר
שָׁמַיִם נִשְׁפָּכִים כְּחָלָב כֵּהֶה, מָתוֹק.
נְשִׁימוֹת קְטִיפָה מַפְרִיחוֹת עֲנָנִים
עַפְעַף יָרֵחַ נִפְקָח מַעַל.
מֵעֹמֶק הֶעָלִים נוֹשְׁבִים אֵלֵינוּ חֲלוֹמוֹת.
אֵינֶנּוּ עֵרוֹת, אֵינֶנּוּ יְשֵׁנוֹת.

לְגִימוֹתָיהָ שֶׁל בִּתִּי פּוֹעֲמוֹת
כְּלֵב. בַּקָּצֶה הָאֶחָד שֶׁל הַלַּיְלָה הַזֶּה:
הָרִקּוּדִים שֶׁרָקַדְנוּ בָּעֶרֶב,
בַּקָּצֶה הָאַחֵר: הַסִּפּוּרִים
שֶׁעֲדַיִן לֹא סִפַּרְנוּ.

מִסָּבִיבֵנוּ דּוֹרוֹת שְׁקוּפִים
שֶׁל אִמָּהוֹת וּבָנוֹת
שֶׁקָּמוּ וְיָשְׁנוּ אֶת חַיֵּיהֶן בֵּין אוֹר
לְחֹשֶׁךְ, מִשֵּׁנָה לִתְקוּמָה
לְשֵׁנָה, יָלְדוּ זוֹ אֶת זוֹ וְנִשְׁכְּחוּ.

בִּתִּי הִיא שַׁעַר אֶל הַשָּׁחֹר הָרַךְ,
אֶל כָּל מָה שֶׁנּוֹלַדְתִּי
לְהִזָּכֵר בּוֹ מֵחָדָשׁ.

ACKNOWLEDGMENTS

With gratitude to the following journals for publishing the English trans-
lations of the poems listed below, sometimes in earlier versions.

Cagibi: "I Want an Electric Juicer."

Copper Nickel: "Hiding," "My Mother Invites a Doctor to Lunch,"
"Three Years Since Your Death."

Hala: "Come," "My Daughter is the Gateway to the Night," "Rehabilita-
tion," "Wherever We Float."

Hayden's Ferry Review: "It's January Again. What Would I Be Telling
You Now?"

Literary Review of Canada : "Autumn."

The New Quarterly: "Hunger," "Home."

The High Window: "We Return From the Sea," "At the Edge of the World."

RHINO: "Cotton" – Winner of the 2020 RHINO Translation Award.

Words Without Borders: "Freedom."

Zocalo Public Square: "Grace After Meals."

NOTES

The author and translator would like to thank Ayelet Tsabari and Ayelet Rose Gottlieb for their work on early drafts of some of the poems in this collection.

The poem "Memorial" is in conversation with "Hummingbird" by Dorianne Laux.

The poem "Australia" is in conversation with "Surprise" by Carrie Fountain.

"Extinction," "Rome" and "Redemption With the Fall of Evening" appear in Hebrew in *Coping Mechanisms*, Mossad Bialik 2021

A translation into French of "Rehabilitation," "Home," and "My Mother Invites a Doctor for Lunch," appear in the anthology: *Under Our Ruptured Sky.*

AUTHOR AND TRANSLATOR BIOS

Maya Tevet Dayan is the author of a novel *One Thousand Years To Wait* (2011) and three books of poetry: *Let There Be Evening. Let There Be Chaos* (2015), *Wherever We Float, That's Home* (2018) and *Coping Mechanisms* (2021). Tevet Dayan is the recipient of the Israeli Prime Minister award for literature for 2018 and an honorable mention the Kugel Poetry Prize for 2016. English translations of her poems have appeared in *Modern Poetry in Translation, Rattle Magazine, World Literature Today, The New Quarterly* and *Literary Review of Canada.* She holds a PhD in Indian Philosophy and Literature. Her latest book, *Feminism, as I Told it to My Daughters* (2023) is a memoir based on her popular columns published in *Haaretz* magazine. She recently translated into Hebrew a collection of the American poet Dorianne Laux.

Jane Medved is the author of *Wayfarers* (winner of the Off The Grid Prize 2024) and *Deep Calls To Deep* (winner of the Many Voices Project, New Rivers Press 2017) Recent work has appeared in *Bending Genres, Ruminate, The North American Review,* and the anthologies: *Ache: The Body's Experience Of Religion* (Flipped Mitten Press) and *Contemporary Jewish Poetry* (Laurel Review) Other awards include winner of the 2021 RHINO translation prize and the 2021 Janet B. McCabe Poetry Prize – Honorable Mention. Her translations of Hebrew poetry can be seen in *Hala, Hayden's Ferry Review* and *Copper Nickel.* She is the poetry editor of The *Ilanot Review,* and a visiting lecturer in the Graduate Creative Writing Program at Bar Ilan University, Tel Aviv.

Wherever We Float, That's Home was printed in Times New Roman

www.saturnaliabooks.com